Environmental Change

FRED MARTIN

Heinemann

First published in Great Britain by Heinemann Library
Halley Court, Jordan Hill, Oxford OX2 8EJ
a division of Reed Educational & Professional Publishing Ltd

MELBOURNE AUCKLAND
FLORENCE PRAGUE MADRID ATHENS
SINGAPORE TOKYO CHICAGO SAO PAULO
PORTSMOUTH NH MEXICO
IBADAN GABORONE JOHANNESBURG
KAMPALA NAIROBI

Designed by Artistix
Originated by Dot Gradations Ltd., South Woodham Ferrers
Printed in the UK by Jarrold Book Printing Ltd., Thetford

00 99 98 97 96
10 9 8 7 6 5 4 3 2 1

ISBN 0 431 06433 4

British Library Cataloguing in Publication Data

Martin, Fred, 1948 –
    Environmental change – (Themes in geography)
    1. Environmental sciences – Juvenile literature
    2. Environmental protection – Juvenile literature
    I. Title II. Series
    333.7

Acknowledgements
The Publishers would like to thank the following for permission to reproduce photographs.
Ace Photo Library/Benelux Press: p.14. Ace Photo Library/Mike Shirley: p.29. Ace Photo Library/Roger Howard: p.13. Ace Photo Library/T & J Florian: p.17. Bruce Coleman/Adrian Davies: p.37. Bruce Coleman/Michael Freeman: p.9. Christine Osborne Pictures: p.15. Environmental Picture Library/Irene Lengui: p.33. Environmental Picture Library/Mike Jackson: p.32. Environmental Picture Library/Robert Brook: p.40. Frank Lane/E & D Hosking: p.12. Frank Spooner/Gamma/Kuku Kurita: p.25. Fred Martin: p.42. Image Bank/Infocus International: p.30. Image Bank/Paul Trummer: p.24. Katz/Richard Baker: p.22. Magnum/F Mayer: p.28. Magnum/Ian Berry: p.7. Magnum/Stuart Franklin: p.36. Nature Photographers/Robin Bush: p.39. Robert Harding Picture Library: p.43. Robert Harding Picture Library/J Lightfoot: p.21. Robert Harding Picture Library/N Peck: p.16. Robert Harding Picture Library/Paolo Koch: p.34. Still Pictures/B & C Alexander: p.38. Still Pictures/Daniel Dancer: p.11, p.19. Still Pictures/David Drain: p.31. Still Pictures/Mark Edwards: p.5, p.8, p.20, p.23. Still Pictures/Martin Wright: p.35. Still Pictures/Michael Gunther: p.10. Still Pictures/Nigel Dickinson: p.18. Stock Photos/Steve Allen: p.41. Telegraph Colour Library/Dan Ford: p.27. Telegraph Colour Library/L Lefkowitz: p.26. Telegraph Colour Library/Pascal Maitre: p.45. Telegraph Photo Library/A Tilley: p.44. Tony Stone/Hans Peter Marten: p.6. Tony Stone/Jacques Jangoux: p.4.

Cover photograph reproduced with permission of The Image Bank.

Our thanks to Clare Boast, Sutherland Primary School, Stoke on Trent, for her comments in the preparation of this book.

Every effort has been made to contact copyright holders of any material reproduced in this book. Any omissions will be rectified in subsequent printings if notice is given to the Publisher.

Contents

Clearing the land

The first human beings lived by hunting and collecting food. There were very few of them and their way of life did not change the Earth's landscape much. By about 8000 years ago, some of our ancestors had started to grow crops and rear animals. That was the start of farming. Since then, a very large part of the Earth's surface has been changed.

Natural environment

The natural environment of an area is made up of rocks and soil, rivers and lakes, plants and wild animals, combined with the weather conditions. Together, all of these things create an interconnected system.

The soil is made from rocks and the remains of plants. Animals and the weather break down the rocks to make the soil. Without the soil, there would be no plants. Every aspect of a local natural environment depends on the others.

Human environment

People are able to change the environment very quickly. Today, chain saws and bulldozers can clear away trees within minutes. This gives space for farms, houses, roads and other buildings. These are all part of the **human** or **built environment**.

The Amazon rain forest in Brazil.

Rain forest vegetation forms the natural environment in this area.

Native people live in this vast area but their way of life does not change the area much.

A clearing in the Amazon rain forest in Peru.

Rows of crops have replaced the natural forest vegetation.

Changing the landscape

In many countries, there is very little left of the original natural environment. Over the years, land has been cleared of its natural vegetation for farming, industry and settlements.

In the UK, almost all the original forests had already been cleared by 500 years ago. In the USA, the forests and prairie grasslands were chopped down and ploughed up over the last 200 years.

Only the highest mountain peaks and places where it is either too hot or too cold for farming have escaped these changes.

The last forests?

Forests are still being cut down in many parts of the Earth. This happens especially in countries where the population is increasing quickly.

More people means a need for more food and more resources. This is one reason why the rain forests of South America, Africa and south-east Asia are being cut down. Before long, there may be nothing left.

Did you know?

About 1 acre of tropical rain forest is cleared every second.

At least half of all the plant and animal species existing on Earth may live in the tropical rain forests.

Resources from rocks

Many of the things you use are made from rocks. Anything that is metal comes from a rock. The knives and forks you use all come from rocks. Clay that makes bricks, and sand that makes glass, both come from rocks.

Mining and quarrying

The job of digging rocks out of the ground is called mining or **quarrying**. Mining is usually when the rock is underground. A quarry is where the rock is dug out from the surface. An **open cast** mine is when a thin top layer of soil and rock are removed to get at the rock being mined. Mines completely underground are called **shaft** mines.

Using rocks

Blocks of slate and granite are used as building materials. Metals such as iron have to be melted out of the rock. This is called smelting.

Fossil fuels

Rocks are also a source of energy. Coal is burnt to generate electricity. Crude oil found in rocks is **refined** to make fuel for cars, trains, boats and aircraft.

These types of resources are called **fossil fuels**. This is because they are made from the remains of plants and animals that lived on the Earth millions of years ago.

An open cast mine in Germany.

Coal is being mined to be burnt in a power station.

The impact of mining

Mining and quarrying have a big effect on the environment. A large hole is dug out of the ground. This makes a scar in the landscape where the trees and grass used to be.

Work at a mine can mean blasting using explosives. This causes loud noises and clouds of dust. The noise from heavy lorries and other machinery also is hard to hide when so much of the work is in the open air.

There are usually piles of waste rock called **spoil tips** at a mine. Rain runs off these tips taking soil and **pollution** into streams and rivers. This can kill wildlife and make people ill where a poisonous or **toxic** metal is being mined.

Special problems occur in areas where mining is underground. The surface can collapse as rocks below are removed. This is called subsidence.

Restoring land

Modern mines are not always eyesores, especially when most of the work is done underground. Mine buildings can look clean and modern. When mining has finished, the land can be **restored** so that it looks attractive again. Quarries can become lakes. Spoil tips can be planted with trees or flattened and used to make places for leisure and recreation.

*An **oilfield** in Azerbaijan.*

Oil is pumped to the surface by pumps called 'nodding donkeys'.

Oil pollutes the ground in the oilfield. Polluted water is washed into streams and rivers.

Did you know?

The world's largest mine is the Bingham copper mine in Utah. The mine is 770 metres deep and 7.2 km² in area.

More coal is mined in the world than any other type of rock.

Storing water

Every living thing needs water. People cannot live without water to drink, to help grow food and to use as a resource in many other ways. More than enough rain falls every year to give as much as people need. The problem is that it does not always come in the right place and at the right time.

Fresh water

Only 3% of the Earth's water is fresh water. The rest is salt water in the seas and oceans. Most of the fresh water flows down rivers back to the seas. A small amount stays in lakes for a while. Even this continually evaporates or flows out into a river.

Some water trickles down through the soil and into the rocks below. It can stay there as groundwater for many years. Some comes back to the surface more quickly through springs.

Fetching water

In the past, people had to live near a water supply. This was usually a stream, river or well. Many people in the developing world still have to do this. Water has to be fetched in containers and carried home.

Today, it is getting harder to keep the water supply clean and reliable. Water **pollution** has become a serious problem and rising populations mean that more water is needed.

A reservoir in Tanzania.

People use the fresh water both for fishing and as a supply of drinking water.

Water is piped to the cities where people do not have their own local supplies.

The 221 metre high Hoover Dam across the Colorado River in Nevada, USA.

Lake Mead is the largest reservoir in the USA.

Water from the reservoir is needed by people who live in the cities of California.

The water problem

The amount of water in rivers and lakes depends on the weather. One problem is that people use most water when there is least rain. A large and regular supply is also needed in the cities where millions of people live.

A reservoir

One answer to the supply problem is to create lakes called **reservoirs** to store water in. These are often in mountain areas where there is most rain. The idea is to catch the rain and stop it from flowing down the rivers and out to the sea.

A dam is built across a river and a reservoir fills up behind it. Water flows from the reservoir through pipes, or in open canals called **aqueducts**. Water in a reservoir has to be kept clean. This is why boats with engines are not usually allowed on reservoirs.

The cost of water

A dam and reservoir affects the environment in several ways. A whole valley can be drowned as the reservoir fills with water. This can make the area look more attractive.

However, people's homes may be in the valley and they will have to be rehoused. Also, the best farmland is often in the bottom of a valley. This means that water for some people is provided at the expense of problems for others.

Did you know?

In the UK, 84 billion litres of water are used every day.

The largest reservoir in the world is Lake Volta in Ghana. This has filled up behind a dam that was built to generate electricity.

The timber business

Wood has been used to make weapons, build houses, make machinery and to burn as a fuel. Today, wood is still an important resource for making products ranging from paper to furniture.

Types of trees

There are two main types of trees. There are **deciduous** trees such as oak and ash. Deciduous trees have leaves that fall off each year. They grow slowly but have hard wood that lasts well.

The other type of trees are **coniferous** trees. These have needles instead of leaves that usually stay green all year round. Most of them grow much faster than deciduous trees but their wood is usually much softer.

Some types of tree are **native** to each area. This means they suit the local soils and climate so they grow there naturally. Trees are farmed by being planted in **forestry plantations**, when their wood is in demand.

Forestry work

Trees are a natural resource that can be grown again. This makes them an **infinite** resource because it should never run out.

In countries such as Canada and Sweden, there are laws that make sure that most of what is cut down is replaced. New trees are planted in **tree nurseries**. When they have grown a little, they are planted out into the main forests.

Felling trees in the rain forests of central Africa.

Timber is a valuable resource worth lots of money for a poor country.

Felling the forests

Selling wood is a way to earn money. A tree weighing several tonnes can be worth a large amount of money when it is cut into planks and sold as timber. This is why cutting down trees has become an important industry in some countries of the developing world.

Massive areas of tropical rain forest are cut down every year. Trees such as teak and ebony have very hard wood that looks attractive and is used for making furniture. In the USA, forests are also being **clear felled**. This means a whole area is cleared of trees.

A problem is that the trees are not always replanted. The amount of the Earth covered in forest goes down every year in many places. Soon there may be none left.

Landscapes without trees

A landscape without trees soon changes. Rain falls directly on the ground and washes away the soil. Without soil, nothing can grow. This is called **soil erosion**. Soil washes into rivers and clogs them up. This helps cause floods.

Even the climate can be changed. Rain that used to fall on the tree leaves and evaporate back to the air, flows away down the rivers. With less evaporation there is less water in the air, so the amount of rain becomes less.

A clear-felled area in Washington, USA.

Hill slopes are left bare as trees are removed.

Clear felling changes the area's soil, wildlife, rivers and even the local climate.

It is almost impossible to regrow a whole forest to its natural state.

Did you know?

Thailand lost 33% of its tropical rain forest between 1963 and 1993.

The new countryside

The countryside can look as if it has never changed. Fields and farm houses seem to have been there for ever. But ways of farming and the types of food grown are always changing. These differences bring changes to the farming landscape.

Bigger fields

By the start of the 1900s, farmland in much of the UK was a patchwork of small fields. These were surrounded by stone walls or by hedgerows.

The farm landscape began to change as farm machinery such as tractors and combine harvesters became larger and more powerful. Many of the hedgerows were dug up to make the fields bigger. Ponds were filled in as farms got their water from pipes.

Loss of wildlife

Hedgerows and ponds are important **habitats** for country wildlife. Birds, insects and small mammals such as field mice live in hedgerows, which they use as safe routeways for travel. A varied landscape with hedgerows can also look better than large open fields.

Trees, disease and storms

Sometimes it is nature that causes changes. In the 1970s, 25 million elm trees in the UK were destroyed by Dutch elm disease.

Storm force winds in 1989 knocked down millions of trees in the south of England. It will take many years to replace them.

A hedgerow is being dug out by a digger.

Some hedgerows have been part of the countryside landscape for hundreds of years.

Hedgerows are the habitats for many species of wildlife.

Farms and fertilizers

Farmers used to keep their fields **fertile** by letting the land rest between crops and by spreading animal manure on them. Now, most fields are given chemical fertilizers and pesticide sprays against pests and crop diseases. Farmers hope that this will not cause problems for the soil in the future.

Golf on the farm

Farmers in the European Union (EU) countries often produce more than can be sold. Now there are rules to make farmers produce less. Fields are either left without crops as **set-aside**, or used for another purpose. Some farmers have turned their fields into golf courses or other types of recreation area.

Farmers find it more profitable to grow large amounts of the same crop in large fields.

Did you know?

Since 1950, 200,000 km of hedgerows in the UK have been dug up. This is almost half way from the Earth to the Moon!

In August 1995, the EU countries agreed to destroy thousands of tonnes of unwanted food. The farmers had produced too much again.

New land

People need land for many of the things they do. Farmers need land to grow crops and rear animals. Land is needed for factories, shops, offices, roads and airports. It is often hard to find the right amount of land in the right place. The answer may be to make more!

Dutch polders

The Netherlands is one of the world's smallest countries. It is also one of the world's most densely populated countries. This means there is a shortage of land for farming, settlements and everything else.

One way to get more farm land is to drain marshes and lakes.

The Dutch also make dry land out of the sea. This is called land **reclamation**.

Land is reclaimed by building a wall called a **dyke** around the area to be reclaimed. Then the water is pumped out until the ground is dry. These places are called **polders**.

Estuary land

New land is also needed for factories and docks. Areas of sea and marsh have been drained along river estuaries such as the Thames and Rhine. Flat land near the sea is ideal for factories that transport goods by ship and need a large amount of space.

The Dutch town of Willemstad and the surrounding polder landscape.

Dykes protect the polders from flooding.

New fields in the desert of Abu Dhabi.

There are sand dunes in the background.

A supply of water from under the ground is used to grow crops on this land that was desert.

Farming dry lands

Many parts of the Earth are too dry for farming for part or all of the year. Most dry areas could be farmed if the land was watered. Putting water on the land is called **irrigation**.

There are many farms in the USA and Australia that depend on irrigation. Some of the profits from this type of farming have to go to pay for the cost of storing and transporting the water.

Tokyo's new airport

In Japan, only 15% of the land is low lying and flat. Almost all of this flat land has already been built on. The only way to get more land is to reclaim it from the sea.

In 1994, a new airport for Tokyo was opened in Osaka Bay. There was nowhere else to build it.

Did you know?

About 25% of The Netherlands is polderland, below sea level.

A new airport is to be built for Hong Kong. Land for the airport will be on land to be reclaimed from the sea. The new airport will cost at least £13 billion to build.

The airport needed flat land that was away from where people lived. Part of the bay had to be filled in using the rock from two mountains. The airport is set to become one of the busiest in Asia. About 23 million passengers a year will soon be passing through it.

Urban environments

About half the people on Earth live in towns and cities. In some countries, such as the UK and the USA, about eight out of every ten people live in towns and cities. These are called **urban** areas. Soon, more than half the Earth's population will be living in urban environments.

Cities, drains and rivers

Cities cover large areas with concrete, brick and other hard surfaces. This affects what happens to rainwater. Rain does not sink through these surfaces so drains are needed instead.

Rainwater quickly flows through drains and into rivers. This can add to the risk of a flood. Rivers that flow through urban areas have to be controlled to stop them from flooding. High banks and dams are built to hold back the water.

Nature in the city

There is some vegetation in urban areas. There are trees, grass and flowers in people's gardens and in parks.

There are also special types of urban wildlife. Birds such as pigeons make their homes in buildings and on window ledges. In some British cities, foxes live by hunting and eating refuse. They stay hidden during the day and come out at night.

Part of an inner city district of New York City, USA.

The natural drainage, climate and wildlife are all affected by the city's buildings, traffic and streets.

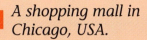

A shopping mall in Chicago, USA.

The climate and light are controlled in this artificial environment.

'Islands' of heat

An urban area can change the local climate. Concrete and brick absorb more heat from the sun than grass and soil. The buildings themselves are heated and some of the heat escapes. Car and lorry engines also give out more heat.

The result is that cities are a few degrees warmer than land in the surrounding countryside. This is called an 'urban heat island'. At night in winter, it can be 8°C warmer in a city than in surrounding countryside.

The air itself is being changed by cities. Pollution from cars, homes and factories rises from exhausts and chimneys. This can cause **acid rain** and other effects on the world's climates.

An artificial climate

People in cities are often protected from the weather. Shopping is done in shopping malls and superstores. Homes and places of work are heated and can be **air conditioned**. A baseball stadium in Toronto has a roof that covers 3.2 hectares. In the future, people protected like this may stop talking so much about the weather because it really won't affect them.

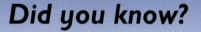

Did you know?

Almost half the energy used in the UK is to heat buildings. Much is wasted due to poor insulation.

Rising hot air over a city can cause clouds and heavy rainstorms.

The Urban Fox Project was started in the UK in 1990. Its aim is to give advice to people who have problems with foxes in cities. The project deals with 4000 phone calls each year.

Transport landscapes

People need to travel and to move goods from place to place. There are many ways that these things can be done. Each of these ways takes up space and affects the environment.

On the roads

Major roads radiate out from big cities like spokes in a wheel. In the UK, the widest roads are the motorways. Motorways are built in giant sweeping curves so traffic does not have to slow down too much.

Land is used to build motorway service stations with car and lorry parks, petrol pumps, restaurants, shops and motels. Roundabouts at access points take up even more space.

On the rails

Trains also need a large amount of space. Railway wagons are shunted into **sidings** where they can be loaded and unloaded.

Goods can be moved in large boxes called containers, which are lifted by a special crane straight from a railway wagon to a lorry.

Port scenes

Ships bring goods from other countries. These are called **imports**. Goods sent to other countries are called **exports**.

Space with special facilities on the **quay** is needed for the ships to dock and the goods to be handled. There are cranes, warehouses and stockpiles to move and store the goods. Facilities are also needed to fuel and repair ships.

There are **customs** buildings and offices where all the paperwork is filled in. All this work creates an area known as **dockland**.

A major airport

A large jet aircraft needs a runway that is flat and at least 3 km long. Most large airports are so busy that they need more than one runway.

Runways often lie in different directions. This is because it is best for aircraft to land and take off into the direction of the wind. The wind does not always blow from the same direction.

Hangars for aircraft repair, a **terminal building** for passengers and **freight sheds** for cargo are all needed, as well as car park space.

Did you know?

The UK motorways are less than 1% of all the roads, but they take 15% of all the road traffic.

A port scene in the state of Washington, USA.

A ship uses its own cranes to load logs for export.

Landscapes for leisure

People in the world's wealthy countries are spending more time and money on leisure. There are more facilities for activities such as sport, entertainment and hobbies. More holidays are spent in distant places. The right kind of environment is needed so that people can enjoy themselves.

Sun seekers

A holiday in the sun is a treat for people who live in places where the holiday weather is unreliable. This is why more than 100 million people go to the coast and islands in the Mediterranean Sea every year. This is also why Florida and California in the USA have become so popular for holidays.

Making a resort

All along the Mediterranean coast, fishing villages have been changed into busy seaside resorts. Now hotels and blocks of apartments line the coast.

Airports and new roads have been built. People need to have easy access to their holiday resort. Everything that visitors want is provided. When nature has not provided a beach, sand can be brought in by lorry. A new harbour can be built where the coast is not sheltered.

These changes can spoil the area's natural environment and cause **pollution**. They also bring jobs.

A leisure complex on the Adriatic coast, Italy.

This is one of the world's most popular seaside areas.

The sea is heavily polluted with sewage from the hotels.

The DisneyWorld theme park in Orlando, Florida, USA.

DisneyWorld was opened in 1971. The site covers 43 square miles.

Did you know?

The world's top three countries for holidays are the USA, France and Spain.

About 10 million people visit EuroDisney near Paris each year.

About 1 million visitors from other countries go to Florida for a holiday each year.

Theme parks

A theme park is another place to spend some leisure time. The theme can be a special period of history, a story or somewhere in the world.

The most well known theme parks are those to do with Walt Disney's cartoons. DisneyLand in California was the first of these. There are also Disney theme parks in Florida, Tokyo and near Paris.

World of fantasy

A theme park is a world where almost anything is possible. Roller-coaster rides take you on journeys through dangerous places. You can live through an earthquake or travel through a crocodile swamp. Whole streets are built to take you to another time or another place.

The environment is controlled by electronics and a network of tunnels under the ground. It is an environment of fantasy.

Dirty air

It is not safe to breathe in some of the world's biggest cities. The problem is caused by smoke and chemicals in the air. This is called air **pollution**. In Tokyo, London and Los Angeles, it is not unusual to see people wearing dust filters over their mouths and noses as they walk or cycle to work.

Burning fossils

Most air pollution is caused by burning **fossil fuels** such as coal, oil or petrol. This is what is burnt in most electricity power stations and in vehicles.

Pollution is caused by the chemicals in the fuel that are not completely burnt. Small pieces escape and go into the air.

Some of these are tiny pieces of sulphur and lead. There are also gases such as carbon dioxide and carbon monoxide. Mixed together, they form a mix of pollution that is called **smog**.

Smog cities

Some cities are more affected by smog than others. Polluted air can be trapped over low ground if the air above is slowly sinking. This is what happens in Denver and Los Angeles in the USA. The pollution cannot rise and escape, so it builds up and becomes even more dense.

Smog is so bad in parts of California that from 1996, at least 2% of all new cars sold must be pollution-free.

A power station in Nottinghamshire, UK.

Steam from the giant cooling towers is harmless, but the power station burns coal to generate electricity.

More air pollution comes from vehicles on the nearby main road.

A health hazard

The effect of smog on people's health can be serious. Lungs can become infected and cause attacks of asthma. Lead affects the blood and brain. Chemicals and tiny pieces of dust can build up and cause cancers. This can happen when people breathe in tiny pieces of asbestos fibre. Asbestos was widely used in buildings for insulation until it was discovered that it was dangerous.

Acid rain

Some chemicals such as sulphur are mixed with water when it rains. This makes the **acid rain** that can eat into stone, destroy trees and kill fish.

Destroying ozone

In 1985, a scientist discovered that a layer of gas in the atmosphere was being destroyed over Antarctica. This is the ozone layer. It stops the sun's harmful rays from reaching the Earth. This layer is being destroyed by chemicals such as those used in aerosol sprays. Use of these chemicals is now banned in many countries.

Did you know?

Amounts of acid are measured on the pH scale. Rain over industrial areas in the northeast USA sometimes has a pH value of 4.1. This is many times more acidic than normal rainwater at pH 5.6.

Plants and animals in Sweden are being killed by acid rain from UK and German power stations.

Lime is spread on the surface of the lake to make the water less acidic.

A load of rubbish

Everyone makes waste. There is waste material created every time a sweet is eaten or a can of drink is opened. The problem then is what to do with the waste.

Types of waste

About 20 million tonnes of waste is collected from homes in the UK each year. That is almost one third of a tonne for each person. This is only 5% of the country's waste. The rest, making a total of 400 million tonnes, comes from mining, farming and industry.

Much of the domestic waste comes from packaging. Some packages are needed to keep goods safe or clean. Others are only to help sell the product. All of it is thrown away when the product is opened and used.

In the USA, 40% of all domestic waste is paper. Other materials such as plastics, glass and metals are each around 10% of the total.

Places for waste

In the UK, 90% of domestic waste is put into **landfill sites**. In the USA, the figure is 73%. Some of the rest goes into **incinerators** where it is burnt.

In a crowded country such as the UK, it is becoming hard to find enough space to dump all our rubbish. Old quarries are sometimes used, but new dumps are needed as these are filled up. Some rubbish has to be moved by train from one county to another for disposal. The problem in the USA is much the same. By the year 2000, one third of all the landfill sites will already be full.

A waste dump in Tokyo, Japan.

The rubbish is making new land by filling in part of Tokyo Bay.

It won't rot

In time, some types of waste rot and break down. These are usually **organic wastes** such as waste food. This can be used as a garden fertilizer.

There is also a large amount of waste that does not break down so easily. Car tyres from millions of cars are thrown away every year. These are made from rubber and synthetic materials that are supposed to last, so they do not break down easily. Plastic bottles are also hard to destroy. Burning tyres and plastic is not the answer as this causes yet more air pollution.

Dangerous rubbish

Some waste is dangerous. Used oil and chemicals are sometimes dumped where they can leak into rivers and water supplies.

Paper and cans are often dropped on the ground as litter. This makes a place look untidy. At worst, it can provide a comfortable breeding place for pests like rats and insects.

In country areas, litter such as sharp and rusty cans can kill wildlife such as foxes and smaller mammals such as voles and mice. Plastic bags can also kill wildlife if they eat or crawl into them.

Did you know?

In the USA every year, 230 million car tyres are dumped.

One incinerator in California burns car tyres to make electricity for 15,000 homes.

A waste tip of scrap metal in Iceland.

The metal slowly rusts and breaks down.

Water: Earth's life blood

To be of any use, water has to be clean. Polluted water brings nothing but problems.

Factories, mines and homes

Some factories use rivers as drains for their waste. This is against the law in many countries. **Pollution** also comes from old mines that have been flooded. About 600 km of rivers in the UK are polluted by water from old coal and metal mines.

Homes create pollution in the form of human waste, which is known as sewage. Most sewage gets some treatment to clean it up. Unfortunately, some does get pumped untreated into the sea.

Farms and pollution

Farms can cause water pollution. Fertilizers such as nitrates and phosphates are used to make crops grow better. Chemicals are sprayed on crops to prevent disease and to kill insects.

These can then be washed into the rivers by heavy rain. Waste **slurry** from pigs and cattle is also washed into rivers.

Chemicals and animal slurry increase the number of **microbes** in the water. They take up oxygen and make **algae** grow. Without oxygen, fish and other species soon die.

Pollution in a river has caused the orange scum.

It is sometimes hard to find out where the pollution has come from.

Pollution in groundwater

Some pollution sinks through the ground under **landfill sites**. Dangerous chemicals in metal drums are sometimes dumped in this way. The chemicals leak when the drum splits open or rusts.

The pollution becomes part of the groundwater stored in rocks. In the end, it seeps out through springs and flows into the rivers. People can add to the problem when oil from car engines is changed and the old oil is thrown away.

Passing it on

Pollution in water spreads quickly. It is almost impossible to stop this happening.

Small pieces of metals such as lead, cadmium, mercury and arsenic float down the river Rhine from factories in Germany. This passes through The Netherlands then flows out to the North Sea. The metals then make some North Sea fish unsafe to eat.

Tanker accidents, such as the *Braer* in 1993, spill thousands of tonnes of crude oil into the sea. This floats on the surface until it is washed ashore. Sea birds, fish and other animals are killed when this happens.

An oil spill at sea when an oil tanker caught fire.

The oil floats on top of sea water and causes an oil slick.

Did you know?

A cow produces about 2$\frac{1}{2}$ tonnes of dung each year.

In 1995, about 135 kg of fertilizers were used on every hectare of farm land in the UK. The figure for 1970 was only 100 kg. In the USA, 36 kg were used in 1970 and about 43 kg in 1995.

Look out!

Road signs along Route 66 in the USA.

Adverts for roadside businesses add to the clutter of information.

Most people know what type of scenery they like. There are also varied things that people think are boring or even ugly. People have different ideas so it is hard to keep the environment looking attractive for everyone.

Buildings

Buildings are the most obvious features in a town landscape. These are designed by **architects** who often have interesting ideas about how buildings should look.

Some want their buildings to stand out and be seen. They do this by building higher, using bright colours, different materials and by building shapes that are unusual.

Others prefer buildings that look like other nearby buildings. This can be done by using similar shapes, colours and designs to what was there before. A building which looks out of place is sometimes called an eyesore.

Street signs

Streets can look unattractive because of road signs and adverts. Some information is needed to show motorists where to go, but too much information can be confusing and an eyesore. In the UK, permission is needed from a planning department of the local council before an advert can be put up near a road.

Power overhead

Some features cannot help standing out in a landscape. Electricity transmission cables and pylons stand out clearly in a flat landscape of fields and woods. Their stark shapes are unnatural against the more natural shapes and colours of the countryside.

Transmission lines can be hidden by putting them under ground. This is very expensive to do and makes it more difficult to make repairs.

Changing views

Changes to the landscape can mean new jobs and a better standard of living for people who live in the countryside. A new factory or new houses may look unattractive, but may be needed by the local people.

A problem is that people's ideas about what is attractive keep changing. Buildings that were once thought to be ugly are now being preserved. Perhaps today's eyesores will be preserved in the future.

Did you know?

There are over 7000 km of overhead transmission cables in the UK. These are part of the national grid that links about 70 power stations to people's homes and to businesses.

Overhead electricity transmission cables and pylons in Kent, UK.

The view from the house is affected by the size and shape of the pylons and cables.

Smelly, noisy neighbours

Noise may be a sound that you do not want to hear. A nasty smell can also be a nuisance. Noise and smells are a part of the environment that is as important as what is seen. A special problem is that they are carried from place to place by the wind.

Measuring noise

Noise is measured in units called **decibels**. A noise meter is used to do this. A large jet aircraft taking off makes a noise of up to 110 decibels.

Aircraft noise

One of the noisiest places to live is directly under the flight path approaching the runway of a major airport. Aircraft suddenly swoop in low as they land. Jet engines make a loud whining sound as they approach the runway.

The engines are at their loudest during take-off. At least they get high into the air quickly. This keeps some of the noise away from people who live nearby.

Lines called noise contours can be drawn to show the area with the greatest noise. The area inside the contours is called a noise 'footprint'.

A modern jet aircraft on the flight path towards a major UK airport.

Most flights are banned from late at night until the early morning because of the noise nuisance.

Roads and railways

Living near a main road or motorway brings a different kind of noise. Car and lorry engines make a constant rumbling noise during the day. Even at night, some roads are also still busy. Embankments help muffle traffic noise.

Noise from trains is louder, but is less frequent. Noise from high-speed trains comes as a sudden roar and rush of wind. This can cause windows to rattle and buildings to shake.

Some people get used to road and rail noises. Others have to buy double glazing for their windows so they can sleep.

Stop that smell

Some smells make life unpleasant for people. Unlike noise, it is very hard to measure a smell. This does not stop it being a nuisance to people who live near.

It is very hard to stop a smell escaping from a farm or a factory. The smell of animal **slurry** from a farm or chemicals from an oil refinery are hard to get used to.

The only answer to a bad smell may be to shut the business down. This is a problem when people's jobs may be at risk.

Did you know?

Aircraft that break noise limits at London's Heathrow and Gatwick airports have to pay a fine.

These building works cause noise and nuisance for people who live by a main road.

The oceans' resources

Oceans cover about three quarters of the Earth's surface. They contain a vast amount of plant and animal life and are a valuable resource. In spite of their size, the ocean environments are being changed.

Hunted to extinction

Some animals in the seas are in danger of becoming **extinct**. Whales have been hunted **commercially** for hundreds of years. There are about 70 different types of whale. The blue whale is the biggest mammal, but only about 1000 are still alive.

It is not necessary to hunt whales any more. Other resources can be used instead. This is one reason why, in 1986, most countries agreed not to hunt any more whales.

Japan and Norway still kill some whales. They say this is to help them carry out scientific research, but many other countries say it is unnecessary and don't want them to continue.

There's a catch

Some types of fish are also at risk. Fishing boats now use radar and have longer, deeper nets to catch fish. Already there are signs that there is overfishing. Stocks of fish such as cod in the North Sea are already very low.

Conserving fish for the future will only be successful if there are strict limits on the amount and the size of the fish that can be caught. These limits are called quotas.

A trawler in the North Sea.

Many trawlers have gone out of business as fish stocks have gone down.

The Great Barrier Reef along the east coast of Australia.

The reef is about 2000 km long. Over 350 species of coral live there.

It has taken 600 million years to grow.

Coral reefs

Coral reefs are among the most beautiful places on Earth. They take up 0.2% of the ocean floor but provide a habitat for 25% of the world's sea creatures.

The reef is an underwater structure made from the skeletons of different types of coral animals. Each type of coral has a different name which comes from their shape, such as brain coral and antler coral. The reef is a mixture of living coral and the remains of dead coral.

Coral reefs are a **habitat** for many types of tropical fish. They also help break up waves as they approach an island or the coast. This is important in places where there are tropical storms.

Reefs at risk

Some coral reefs are being slowly destroyed. Tourists who come to see them bring **pollution** with motor boat engine oil. Pieces are broken off as souvenirs and trampled on at low tide when they are exposed.

It takes hundreds of years for a few centimetres of coral to grow. It takes only a few seconds for it to be destroyed.

Did you know?

In 1900, about 3 million tonnes of fish were caught in the world. By 1990, this had risen to about 80 million tonnes.

About 90% of coral reefs around the world have already been damaged.

National Parks

Nothing changes a landscape faster than people. In some places, change needs to be slowed down, managed better, or even stopped altogether. One way to do this is to conserve an area as a **National Park**.

National Park landscapes

There are National Parks in many countries such as the UK, USA and France. A National Park is a large area where the landscape, wildlife and natural vegetation are **conserved**. For example, Yosemite National Park in the USA is 3340 km^2 in size.

In the UK, most of the National Parks are in mountain areas. The Snowdonia National Park in the Cambrian mountains of Wales is one example.

In the USA, many National Parks are also in mountain areas. Some, such as the Everglades in Florida are in lowland areas.

Most National Parks have something special that is worth conserving. In Exmoor, there are red deer living in the wild. Yellowstone National Park in Wyoming has the Old Faithful hot water geyser and grizzly bears.

The impact of people

Some National Parks are popular places to visit for a day trip or for a longer holiday. In the UK, about 10 million visitors come to the Lake District National Park every year.

A grizzly bear in the Yellowstone National Park in Wyoming, USA.

National Parks are the only places left where some types of wildlife are safe.

The Lake District National Park in Cumbria, UK.

Walking is a popular activity in the Lake District.

Footpaths are easily worn down by ramblers and by heavy rain.

Visitors change the landscape in several ways. Roads become congested with traffic. Footpaths are worn down and get wider. Facilities are needed such as campsites, toilets and car parks. People also bring noise, litter and pollution.

Managing people

It is hard to provide so many facilities for so many people without damaging the actual environment that the visitors have come to see. Doing this needs good **management**.

Clear signposts are needed to show people where they can and cannot walk. Footpaths can be made to last by laying down stones. Some facilities can be hidden by planting more trees. Strict planning controls can stop buildings and land from being changed too much.

It is hard to get the balance right between conservation and allowing visitors to enjoy the National Parks. This is a problem that will become more difficult in the future.

Did you know?

Yellowstone National Park gets its name from yellow sulphur that stains the rocks. The sulphur comes from volcanic rocks that heat the hot water geysers.

Lake Windermere in the Lake District National Park is England's longest lake. It is 17 km long.

Saving habitats

It seems that nature cannot look after itself any more. There are just too many people. Birds and other types of wildlife are being threatened as their habitats are destroyed. Some endangered animals are still being hunted.

A Game Park in Kenya, Africa.

Herds of zebra, wildebeest, elephants and gazelle can be seen in these Game Parks.

Nature reserves

One way to **conserve** wildlife is to set aside an area as a **nature reserve**. This is being done in Africa where there are very large areas called **Game Parks** and National Parks. The Serengethi National Park in Tanzania is one of the biggest of these at 38,200 km^2. Shooting the animals is only allowed with a camera!

Managing wildlife

The numbers of wild animals in a Game Park has to be kept under control. Too many elephants, for example, can destroy the environment they need as well as harming other species. This is why game wardens sometimes shoot some of the animals. This is called **culling** a herd. The future for all the animals is made safe by doing this.

UK special sites

In the UK, wildlife is being conserved in National Parks and also in much smaller sites. These are called **Sites of Special Scientific Interest** (SSSIs). Species such as butterflies, insects, birds and rare plants are conserved on these sites.

Saving the wetlands

Natural wetlands are one type of **habitat** that are at risk. These areas are also called **fens**.

Wetlands are usually low-lying areas where there is shallow water with beds of reeds and other water-loving vegetation. These areas provide a habitat for many types of birds, insects, frogs and fish.

Some wetlands are on flat land near to sea level. The Somerset Levels in the UK are like this. Others are along the coast where the tide washes over them every day.

Many wetlands have been drained by farmers because the land was needed for houses and factories. Now farmers in the UK are asked not to drain any more wetlands. Instead, the government gives them money to make up for what they could have earned from their land.

Conserving a small wetland area in Surrey, UK.

About half of all fen areas in the UK have been drained since 1945.

Friendly farming

It is sometimes hard to know just what we are eating. Most food is grown in fields sprayed with chemical fertilizers and insecticides. Animals are reared in buildings where the heat, light and the exact amount of food is tightly controlled. The food is processed in a factory to give it more colour, extra flavour and to make it last longer. Not everyone is happy that this is how food is produced.

Chemicals and food

Some people think it is wrong to rely on chemicals to produce our food. This may ruin the soil for the future. Chemicals also cause **pollution** problems when they flow off the fields and into rivers.

Some shoppers are worried. They do not like the idea that animals are badly treated. They also fear that the chemicals may be bad for human health.

Free-range animals

There are about 30 million hens and about 600 million broiler chickens in the UK. Almost nine out of every ten eggs come from hens that live in **battery cages**. Most of the country's 8 million pigs are also reared indoors.

A small number of animals are reared in more natural open conditions. These methods are known as **free range**. Some people feel that this is a better way to treat the animals, and a way to produce better quality food.

Rearing pigs on an organic farm in Dorset.

Pigs are often reared in sheds where living conditions are cramped. Free-range pigs feed in the open in a more natural way.

A meadow of wild flowers and grasses in Oxfordshire.

Most farmers have ploughed up these meadows and planted them with crops or other types of grass.

The organic way

In the past, farmers did not have chemical fertilizers and insecticides. They relied on animal manure to make the fields more fertile. Fields were also rested so that the nutrients needed could be replaced naturally.

Growing crops without using chemicals is called **organic farming**. Farmers who use these methods run the risk of crop diseases and attack by insects. However, they do not have to pay the cost of the chemicals.

Be sensitive

Farmers have always changed the countryside. Now there are very few places left where wildlife and wild flowers still grow.

In the UK, some farmers are now paid to farm in a way that helps to conserve the environment.

Did you know?

Since 1945, 94% of all the UK's lowland grass and herb meadows have been destroyed.

Places with special wildlife and vegetation are made **Environmentally Sensitive Areas** (ESAs). Farmers farm these places in ways that do not harm the environment.

The cost of food

At the moment, organic food is usually more expensive than food grown with chemicals. This is because not as much can be grown. The cost of organic food could become cheaper if the cost of chemicals goes too high or if more people change to eating organic products.

Land restored

It is often very easy to destroy something. It is not so easy to mend it again. The landscape too is easy to destroy. Making it attractive again takes time, money and a lot of work. Doing this is called land **restoration**.

Restoring waste tips

Mining and industry affects the landscape long after the mining has stopped and the factories have closed down. **Spoil tips** and **slag heaps** are left as eyesores and are sometimes dangerous.

Spoil tips can be made to look more attractive by changing their shape. Bulldozers can make them look better by giving them lower slopes with more natural shapes. Trees and other types of vegetation can be planted so that the landscape looks natural again.

Using holes

Mining and quarrying leaves holes in the ground where the rock has been dug from the surface, or where it has subsided.

Some holes are useful as **landfill sites** for rubbish. Another way to use them is to make lakes for yachts or areas for nature **conservation**.

Some quarries are filled in again. Topsoil is put back on top and the land is put back to farming.

Trees have been planted on old industrial land.

Tubes protect the young trees from animals and from the wind.

New buildings on old industrial land in central Manchester, UK.

The canal has been restored and there is a path alongside it.

Some of the old brick buildings are left as a reminder of the area's history.

Derelict land

Some buildings and land become **derelict**. Some sites are left in this state for years. Most of such land can be cleared to be of use again.

In some places, land is too dangerous to use because chemicals from factories have sunk into the ground. They have to be removed before the land can be restored.

Did you know?

In the UK every year, about 110 million tonnes of waste rock from mining are dumped.

There are about 42,000 hectares of derelict land in the UK.

Some derelict buildings are conserved because of their shape and history. They help give character to an area. They can be rebuilt on the inside, but still look the same on the outside. This is called **renovation**.

Railways and canals

Disused railway lines quickly become overgrown with weeds. Some have now been cleared and are used as long-distance footpaths and cycle tracks.

Until recently, most of the UK's canals were disused. Now, the mud is being dug out and the locks are being repaired. This helps make them popular places for recreation.

Saving the Earth

Finite resources

Some of the resources we use are **finite**. Oil, coal and metals are resources that one day will run out. Before that happens, they may become too expensive to mine and to buy.

Some oil and natural gas already comes from very difficult environments. There are **oilfields** and gasfields beneath the sea and from places inside the Arctic Circle in the USA and Russia. There is a very high cost to getting oil and gas from such difficult environments.

Running out

Reserves of oil and gas will be used up in your lifetime in some places. There will be no reserves of oil and gas in some of the North Sea fields in 20 years' time. Geologists are now looking for new reserves in deeper and more dangerous water.

A collecting point for waste in San Francisco, USA.

Materials such as glass, paper and cans can all be recycled. This is one way to help save oil, gas and other sources of energy.

Scrap metal on a dock waiting to be melted down and re-used.

Cars and other metal goods are compressed into small cubes. The metal can be recycled to make new cars.

Recycling

Recycling is one way to make resources last longer. Scrap metal can be melted down and used. Old paper, bottles and clothes can all be re-used instead of using new raw materials.

Did you know?

The 10.30AM Concorde flight from Heathrow lands at New York's JFK Airport at 9.30AM on the same morning. This is twice as fast as any other passenger aircraft. It is also the way that uses most fuel for every passenger that is carried.

Renewable resources

Some resources will only last if they are replaced or used more carefully. Trees, for example, can be replanted to make them an **infinite** resource.

Some types of energy resources do not need to be replaced. Energy from the sun, from the wind and from waves is always available. There is also energy from hot rocks inside the Earth. These are called **renewable** resources.

All these natural sources of energy can be used to generate electricity instead of burning coal, oil and gas. Using these renewable resources will help **conserve** the finite resources for longer.

Environmental action

There is always something that everyone can do to help look after the Earth's environment. Every little bit helps, no matter how small or how big.

Find out

One way to start looking after the environment is to find out how it works. It is easy to destroy a part of the environment without understanding why.

Water is wasted when a tap is left running. Energy is wasted if doors and windows are left open when the heat is on. These kinds of waste can lead to more land being needed for **reservoirs** and more energy resources.

Labels on the goods you buy tell you how they were made and what is in them. Some say they are more friendly to the environment.

Play a part

Some people join organizations that are concerned about the environment. Three of the best known of these are Friends of the Earth, Greenpeace and the Worldwide Fund for Nature. They raise money and work to help improve the environment in places all over the world.

Cleaning litter from a beach.

People of all ages can play a part in improving the environment.

A tree-planting scheme in Burkina Faso, Africa.

Trees help stop the areas from becoming desert.

People have a better standard of living with a better environment.

Keep watch

Watch out for changes in your own neighbourhood. Politicians make decisions about changes to the environment. They need to know what people want so make sure that your opinions are known. It is easy to send a letter about anything you think is important.

Go global

There are books, television programmmes and computer programs with information from all over the world about the environment. People are now able to exchange information and ideas on computer links such as the **Internet**.

Changes to the environment in one part of the world can cause changes in other places. This is why environmental change has to be so carefully understood and planned. Everyone has a part to play.

Useful addresses

Friends of the Earth
26–28 Underwood Street
London, N1 7JQ
Tel: 0171 490 1555

Worldwide Fund for Nature
Panda House, Weyside Park
Godalming, Surrey, GU7 1XR
Tel: 01483 426 444

Greenpeace
Canonbury Villas
London, N1 2PN
Tel: 0171 354 5100

Glossary

acid rain rain which contains a level of acids above that found in normal rainwater

air conditioning control of temperature and air quality in a building

algae a simple type of water vegetation

aqueducts a channel to carry water

architects people who design houses and other buildings

battery cages small cages used to rear chickens

clear felled area of forest completely cleared of trees

commercially for profit

coniferous a tree with needles and cones

conserving/conservation protecting from danger or destruction

culling killing animals to control their numbers

customs the control of imports and exports

decibel the unit used to measure noise

deciduous a tree with leaves that fall off during a cold season

derelict unused land left in a ruined condition

dockland the land around a harbour where there are factories and warehouses

dyke a wall around a reclaimed area

Environmentally Sensitive Areas farming areas in the UK that have some special wildlife and vegetation that is worth conserving

extinct when a species dies out

export to send something out of a country

fens a wetland area with vegetation such as reeds and rushes

fertile (soil) a soil that is good for growing crops

finite does not renew so could run out

forestry plantations large areas of trees planted by people

fossil fuels fuels from rocks such as coal and oil

free range farm animals that are kept in the open air, living in a more natural way

freight sheds buildings at a port or airport where freight is handled and stored

Game Parks large areas where wildlife is conserved

habitat an environment that is the home for particular plants or animals

hangars large buildings for aircraft

human/built environment the landscape that has been created by people

import to bring something into a country

incinerator a building where rubbish is burnt

infinite can renew so will not run out

Internet information links between computers

irrigation watering crops using specially created systems

landfill site a place where rubbish is dumped

management planning how to do or use something or somewhere

microbe very small living organism

National Park a large area of conserved landscape

native a species that has always grown in a particular environment

nature reserve an area where the natural life is conserved

oilfields areas where there is crude oil in the rocks

open cast (mine) digging rocks out of the ground by first removing a surface layer of unwanted rocks

organic farming farming without using artificial chemicals

organic waste waste materials, such as food, that break down naturally

polders a reclaimed area that is often below sea level

pollution hazardous substances in the environment

quarrying digging rocks from the ground on the surface

quay the land beside a harbour where ships tie up

reclamation to make new land, for example from a sea or lake

recycling to use a material again

refined to make more pure, such as changing crude oil to petrol

renewable a resource that can be used again or is always being naturally replaced

renovation to repair and improve

reserves (of supplies) the amount of a particular resource that is left

reservoirs a lake made to store water

restore/restoration to put back to the original use or purpose

set-aside land that farmers in the UK are paid not to use for crops

shaft (mine) an underground mine

sidings an area where trains move wagons, carriages and freight

Sites of Special Scientific Interest sites in the UK where wildlife, plants or rocks are of some special interest

slag heaps heaps of waste rock from metal smelting

slurry animal waste

smog a mixture of fog and air pollution over a city

soil erosion the wearing away of layers of soil

spoil tips heaps of waste rock from mining

terminal building an airport building where passengers start and finish journeys

toxic poisonous to certain living things

tree nursery an area where young trees are first planted

urban to do with towns and cities

Index

Numbers in plain type (17) refer to the text. Numbers in italic type (23) refer to a caption.